Biomes

Wetlands

Duncan Brewer

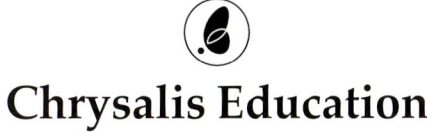

Chrysalis Education

BIOMES

DESERTS
GRASSLANDS
OCEANS
RAIN FORESTS
WETLANDS

US publication copyright © 2003 Chrysalis Education.
International copyright reserved in all countries.
No part of this book may be reproduced in any form
without written permission from the publisher.

Distributed in the United States by
Smart Apple Media
1980 Lookout Drive, North Mankato, Minnesota 56003

Copyright © Chrysalis Books PLC 2003

ISBN 1-59389-126-1

The Library of Congress control number 2003105001

Editor: Andrew Solway
Editorial Manager: Joyce Bentley
Designer: Mark Whitchurch
Consultant: Michael Allaby
Picture Researcher: Glass Onion Pictures

Printed in Hong Kong/China
10 9 8 7 6 5 4 3 2 1

Picture Acknowledgements
We wish to thank the following individuals and organizations for their help and assistance, and for supplying material in their collections: Corbis 7 (NASA), 32 (Lloyd Cluff), 35 (Joe McDonald), 38 (Lloyd Cluff); Digital Vision *front cover*; Ecoscene 6 (Andrew Brown), 15 (W Lawler), 18 (Anthony Cooper), 30 (Paul Ferraby), 34 (Robert Baldwin), 46 (Sally Morgan); FLPA 5 bottom (Roger Tidman), 9 (W Wisniewski), 10 (Sunset), 11 (Eric and David Hosking), 12 (Larry West), 17 (Borrell Casals), 19 (W Wisniewski), 21 (Minden Pictures), 25 (Minden Pictures), 26 (Derek Hall), 37 (Mark Newman), 39 (Michael Gore); NHPA 13 (Anthony Bannister); Oxford Scientific Films 1 (Des and Jen Bartlett), 44 (Des and Jen Bartlett); Panos Pictures 5 top (Chris Stowers), 5 middle (Caroline Penn), 28 (Rhodri Jones), 40 (Betty Press); Rex Interstock 8 (Lars Johnansson); Still Pictures 3 (Gaethlich/UNEP), 4 (Boonsiri/UNEP), 14 (Paul Springett), 16 (Andrew Davies), 20 (Fritz Polking), 22 (Gaethlich/UNEP), 23 (Mark Edwards), 24 (G Griffiths/Christian Aid), 27 (Shehzad Noorani), 29 (Cyril Ruoso), 31 (Roland Seitre), 33 (Ron Giling), 36 (John Cancalosi), 41 (Gerard and Margi Moss), 42 (David Drain), 43 (Mark Edwards), 45 (Joerg Boethling), 47 (Mark Edwards). The pictures used in this book do not show the actual people named in the case studies in the text.

CONTENTS

Boonmee's Story 4

What Is A Wetland? 6

What Are Some Of The Planet's Major Wetlands? 8

What Happens In Wetlands? 10

What Life Depends On Wetlands? 14

Who Are The Wetland Humans? 22

How Do We Benefit from Wetlands? 24

Do Human Activities Endanger Wetlands? 28

How Does Wetland Degradation Affect Wildlife? 34

How Do The Changes To Wetlands Affect Humans? 38

What Are We Doing About Wetland Destruction? 42

Where Do We Go From Here? 46

Reference 48

Glossary 52

Further Information 54

Index 56

Boonmee's Story

Boonmee is a fisherman in Thailand. For almost 10 years, he has been unable to catch enough fish to support his family. Like another 100 million people, his way of life depends on the mighty Mekong River, where new concrete dams are threatening the survival of many fish species. Interference with wetland systems is causing similar problems in many parts of the world.

"WE FISHERMEN KNEW from the beginning that the dam would be a disaster. My village is on the Mun River, a tributary of the Mekong. I used to net and trap some of the fish that swam up the Mun each year to breed in the shallows. When the government announced plans for a new dam on our river, we protested, and explained that we depended on the migrating fish, but they went ahead anyway, and completed the dam in 1994.

The fish usually breed between May and September, but now they are unable to reach the Mun River shallows. Since the dam was built, many fishing families have moved from the village, seeking work elsewhere. I decided to stay on. I joined the remaining villagers to organize protest meetings. For years, we marched and we demonstrated.

The Mekong River supports many thousands of small boat fishermen and their families, but hydroelectric schemes, and the dynamiting of shallows to increase the river's depth, are putting the fishermen out of work.

The government kept telling us the dam would bring us electricity, but what use is that without food?

In 2001, we persuaded the authorities to open the dam's sluice gates for a four-month trial period. The migrating fish immediately began to come upstream again. I took part in a count, which discovered that over 100 species had returned. In 2002, the government agreed to open the sluice gates every year during the fish-breeding season.

I am beginning to catch some fish again, but numbers are still low. I would like to see the dam removed altogether."

How do dams affect wetlands elsewhere?

Dams are one example of the ways in which human activities can affect the people and wildlife dependent on wetlands.

CHINA
The huge Three Gorges Dam is being built on the Yangtze River. It will force well over one million people from their homes and land.

EGYPT
The Aswan Dam on the Nile has stopped the yearly floods that once enriched the lands around the river. Now farmers have to buy chemical fertilizers.

CANADA
Dams built for Quebec's James Bay Project flooded the homes of Cree Indians and caused mercury poisoning in fish and fish-eaters, including humans.

What Is A Wetland?

A wetland is a region where water and land interact. It consists not only of the water and the land, but also of the plants that have adapted to live there. These plants contribute to the way the wetland develops.

Swamp forest trees, such as the bald cypress of the South, often have trunks that are wide at their bases. This helps to stabilize them in the saturated soil where they grow.

THERE ARE MANY different kinds of wetlands, ranging from swamps and mangrove forests in the tropics to peat bogs on windswept mountains. Large wetland areas such as the Florida Everglades, and the Okavango in southern Africa, are famous for their rich and unique mixtures of wildlife.

What is a biome?

A biome is a major regional community of plants and animals, with similar life forms and environmental conditions. Each biome is named after its dominant feature, for example, tropical rainforest or wetland.

What are the different kinds of wetlands?

Marshes: these are among the most common wetlands. They are usually shallow, and support beds of reeds and rushes. They get water directly from springs, rivers, and from regular floods, as well as from rainfall. In river estuaries, there are often areas of salt marsh that are flooded with every tide.

Swamps and swamp forests: these are regions where the soil is saturated with water, and usually flooded. Many exist around the edges of tropical lakes. Swamp forests are dominated by special kinds of trees that grow well in waterlogged soil.

Mangroves: these are forests that fringe the coasts of many tropical countries. They are tidal, so the trees that live there have to be able to grow with their roots in salt water. There are several different families of mangroves. Mangrove forests protect shorelines and support an immense variety of wildlife.

Peat bogs: sometimes dead plant material builds up in waterlogged areas quicker than it can decay. The resulting layer of slowly rotting plant material is known as peat. Peat bogs are wetlands where the peat has built up to a depth of at least 12–16in (300-400mm). They are very acidic, and the soil does not have enough nutrients for most plants. Fens, on the other hand, are peatlands rich in nutrients and low in acidity.

Floodplains: these are lands beside rivers that are flooded regularly in the wet season. They can cover huge areas when the land is particularly flat. Floodplain soils are usually very rich in plant nutrients from the muddy silts deposited by the floodwaters.

A satellite image of the Markham River in Papua New Guinea. It shows how a river's delta is made up of a large number of channels fanning out to meet the sea.

Estuaries, deltas, and tidal flats: these are all regions where rivers enter the sea. They contain some of the planet's most complex wetlands, with regularly changing mixtures of fresh and salt water. An estuary is where a river widens as it joins the sea. A delta is an estuary that has silted up, so that the river fans out into many channels as it joins the sea. Between the channels and lagoons are reed-beds and expanses of tidal mud (tidal flats). The mud in an estuary is rich in nutrients because where fresh and salt water meet, chemicals and nutrient particles cling together and settle on the riverbed.

Lakes: lakes often have wetland systems such as marshes and swamp forests around their shallows. Some lakes have constant inflows and outflows of water, while others have no outlets—they lose water only by evaporation. Lakes of this second kind sometimes become "salt" lakes, because minerals in the lake ("salts") become more concentrated as the water evaporates.

What Are Some Of The Planet's Major Wetlands?

The Florida Everglades consist of grass and sedge marshlands, cypress swamps, and coastal mangroves. They are regularly flooded when Lake Okeechokee in the north overflows, but the flood area has been halved in recent years to accommodate growing human communities.

THE SOUTH AMERICAN Pantanal is one of the Earth's largest floodplains. It covers 77,200 sq mi (200,000 sq km) of Brazil, Bolivia, and Paraguay, and is full of lakes, marshes, streams, and rivers. Floods cover much of the Pantanal in the rainy season, which lasts from December to March, but the floods sometimes continue until mid-June.

The Amazon Basin: this huge basin was created over millions of years by the Amazon River. It covers an area of up to 23,200 sq mi (60,000 sq km), and is a maze of floodplains and lakes. Seasonal floods cover many forest regions with water for months at a time. The enormous Amazon Delta covers an area of 8.6 million acres.

Visitors to the Florida Everglades can explore the winding channels and wildlife of the Wetlands National Park by boat. But outside the National Park area, the wetlands continue to be drained to make way for housing.

8 WETLANDS Biomes

Large elephant herds flourish in Botswana's Okavango region. The area is rich in regularly flooded wetlands, where elephants can drink, bathe, and feed all year without having to migrate vast distances.

The Mekong River and delta: the Mekong stretches 2,600mi (4,200km) from the highlands of Tibet to the South China Sea. Annual floods fertilize agricultural land in five countries on the floodplains beside the river. However, a growing number of dams is disrupting the river's flood cycles.

The Sunderbans: this is the joint delta of the rivers Ganges, Brahmaputra, and Meghna. It contains the world's largest mangrove forest. The tides of the Bay of Bengal flood the streams and channels of the Sunderbans, and the area is probably the most important habitat for the royal Bengal tiger.

The Sudd of Central Sudan: the huge swamps of the Sudd region of Sudan are fed by the White Nile, and form one of Africa's largest floodplains. Many migratory birds and mammals depend on the Sudd as a place to stop off and find food, while local cattle herders depend on its seasonal grasses.

The Okavango: this area in northern Botswana is the world's largest inland delta, where the Okavango River spreads out after being funneled through a natural "panhandle" caused by geological faults. Half the delta is permanent swamp, the rest floods in the rainy season and is grassland at other times. The Okavango contains Africa's largest elephant population.

The Wadden Sea: this is Europe's largest tidal wetland. Protected from the North Sea by the Friesian Islands, the Wadden Sea stretches 310mi (500km) along the coasts of the Netherlands, Germany, and Denmark. It is a combination of islands, sandbanks, salt marshes, and tidal flats. The area is a vital stopover place for migrating birds and fish.

What Happens In Wetlands?

A wetland is constantly undergoing change—growing, shrinking, or altering shape. These changes are affected by the amount of water entering or leaving the wetland and the amount of material carried by the water. Other changes are governed by plant growth and chemical reactions.

IN MOST WETLANDS, the amount of water changes with the seasons. In some places, the river floodplains may show no surface water for most of the year, but are temporarily covered with water when seasonal rains or melting snow cause the rivers to overflow. The permanent swamps of the Sudd region of Sudan cover up to 7,700 sq mi (20,000 sq km), but during the rainy season, the White Nile overflows into the floodplain around the swamps, and adds 5,800 sq mi (15,000 sq km) more to the wetland.

Despite flood-control systems, many European rivers continue to overflow onto their ancient floodplains on a regular basis after heavy rainfalls or snow thaws.

In some floodplains, the water largely disappears between rainy seasons. During the annual monsoon rains in Australia's Northern territory and in Queensland, a number of large streams appear, and flood extensive areas. After the rains have departed, these floods evaporate and sink into the ground, leaving a few swamps and the waterholes known as billabongs.

10 WETLANDS Biomes

What happens in tidal wetlands?

Many rivers flood once or twice each year, but some kinds of wetlands flood much more often. The rise and fall of the tides covers and uncovers many coastal wetlands twice a day, particularly in and around estuary mouths and deltas, where rivers meet the ocean. Sandbanks, mudflats, islands, and salt marshes appear and disappear in coastal wetlands. They are continually changing shape and size as the tides rise and fall. These areas are subject to waves and storm surges as well as regular flooding.

The Mekong Delta, for example, consists of some 21,200 sq mi (55,000 sq km) of freshwater swamp forests, tidal mudflats, and mangroves. After the monsoon rains, floodwater rushing down the river meets with seawater surging upstream. The result is a temporary flood area of up to 131,000 sq mi (340,000 sq km).

The Nine-Dragon river

Mekong means "Nine Dragons," and refers to the nine channels into which the river divides at its delta. The Mekong carries so much water following monsoons that it is higher than some of the smaller rivers feeding into it. Flood surges travel back up these tributary rivers, temporarily reversing their flow. In Cambodia, this reverse flow moves up the Tonle Sap River, and swells the Great Lake upstream to five times its dry season area. After a pause, the flow returns to its normal direction, carrying with it large numbers of lake-breeding fish.

Mudflats on the Severn estuary, UK. With regular inflows of both fresh river water and seawater, the channels and mudflats of a river estuary are constantly changing.

Bogs are often short of the nutrients needed by most plants. Certain plants, such as the sundew shown here, have evolved to survive bog conditions by trapping insects and digesting the nutrients contained in their bodies.

How do wetlands change shape?

Rivers and streams are forever carving and shaping their own beds and edges, removing soil from their banks and carrying it downstream. In addition, they also carry material washed down into them by rainfall. The bigger the river, the more sediment it carries. A flooding river can deposit millions of tons of soil over its floodplain. When it reaches the sea, the river deposits all its remaining sediment. Deltas are built as these sediments are gradually spread along the coast to either side of the river's mouth.

How do lakes become bogs?

Deposits of a different kind can sometimes change lakes into marshes, and marshes into bogs. The process is known as succession. At first mud, gradually washed into a lake by streams, or eroded from the banks, settles on the lake bottom. Eventually, the lake is shallow enough for plants that have floating leaves and flowers to take root. More mud gathers around the roots of these plants, and the lake

Bogs and peat

The decomposition of plant material in marshy areas is a major natural source of methane gas, which contributes toward global warming.

Waterlogging, high acidity, and low oxygen levels are all conditions favorable to peat formation. Such conditions hold back natural decomposition so that it cannot keep up with the amount of material accumulating.

In upland terrains, many bogs are created not on overgrown lakes, but on wet, acidic soils. They are formed by remarkable plants called bog mosses, which can grow on waterlogged ground. These mosses hold on to large amounts of water. This water has absorbed acids from the underlying soil, and the mosses make it more acidic by digesting the nutrients in it.

becomes even shallower. Other plants, known as emergents, take root around the margins. These have most of their stems above water, and are typical marsh plants.

Over the years, silt, and increasing amounts of dead plant material, continue to build up. The new layers begin to solidify, becoming peat, which eventually takes over the whole lake area and turns it into a peat bog.

The Okavango is typical of rivers that form oxbow lakes. It slowly meanders over the flat plains in a series of looping curves, moving through the swamps of the panhandle before spreading over the sands of the Kalahari Desert.

What is an oxbow lake?

In wide, shallow valleys, rivers flow slowly, looping back and forth in a wandering, snakelike path. These snaking curves are called "meanders," after the Menderes River in Turkey. Meanders are formed as erosion wears away the outside of a bend, while eroded material from upstream is deposited on the inside of the bend, emphasizing the curve. Sometimes the neck of one of these loops is eroded away completely, creating a new, straighter course for the river. The old river loop becomes what is known as an oxbow lake. Cut off from the rest of the river, the oxbow lake may eventually dry up completely.

Biomes WETLANDS 13

What Life Depends On Wetlands?

Wetlands are among the world's most vital habitats for plants and wildlife. From tiny insects and fish larvae, to birds and large mammals, many wild animal species are totally dependant on wetlands. Many plants, from microscopic floating species to forest trees, also need wetland conditions in order to survive.

The giant Amazon water lily has leaves that can reach 6ft (2m) across, and can support a weight of up to 100lbs (45kg) without sinking.

DIFFERENT PLANTS GROW in different parts of a wetland. Free-floating plants such as duckweeds colonize open areas of still water such as ponds and lakes, deriving all their nutrients from the water.

Closer to the shore are plants such as waterweed, which root on the bottom, but remain totally submerged. Even closer to the shore is a wide range of bottom-rooting plants with leaves and flowers that float on the surface of the water. These include water lilies and water hyacinths.

The plants of the water margins have their roots in the water or in waterlogged soil, and carry their flowers and seed-heads at the top of long stems. They include reeds, rushes, grasses, and sedges.

Certain plants have adapted to life in wetlands that are low in nutrients by becoming meat-eaters. For example, sundews use sticky hairs to catch their insect prey, and the hairs move inward to hold and digest the insect once it is stuck. Bladderworts are the largest and most widespread group of carnivorous plants. Scattered along the plant's stems and leaves are hundreds or thousands of tiny bladderlike traps, which catch insects and other small creatures.

Can trees grow in water?

Some trees have developed special ways of surviving with their roots permanently in the water. The swamp cypress of North America often occurs in permanently flooded areas, and has large, kneelike extensions to its underwater roots, which rise up out of the water around the trunk. The "knees" trap sediments, to create a solid supporting buttress that stops the tree from toppling over.

Mangroves grow in muddy tidal flats along many tropical coasts, and have developed unique ways of dealing with their marine environment. The photo shows the wide spread of stiltlike roots that support the trees in the tidal mud, and the special breathing roots poking out of the mud into the air.

Mangrove trees also have arching prop roots to support them, but they have other problems to deal with. The mud they grow in is very salty and contains very little oxygen. Some mangrove species get rid of extra salt through their leaves, while others have special cells in the roots that keep the salt from being taken up with the water. Some mangrove species get extra oxygen through tiny pores (holes) in their prop roots. Others send up vertical root growths, which are breathing organs, into the air around the main trunk.

Biomes WETLANDS 15

Every year, many salmon leave the sea and move up rivers to spawn, swimming and leaping their way up torrents and rapids to reach the upper shallows.

Which creatures live underwater?

Forty-one percent of all fish species are found in fresh water, even though fresh water covers only about one percent of the Earth's surface.

Many fish go on spawning migrations: they are born in one wetland area, they migrate to a new area as adults, and then return to their spawning grounds (the area where they were born) to breed. Many Mekong species, for instance, such as the giant Mekong catfish, move from the main river into tributaries, swimming upstream to lay and fertilize their eggs in the shallows.

Can fish live in both fresh and salt water?

Some kinds of fish travel between fresh water wetlands and saltwater oceans. Salmon leave the sea to breed in the freshwater rivers where they were spawned. On the east coast of North America, large schools of alewives, a kind of herring, enter estuaries and swim up rivers and streams to breed in ponds.

Freshwater eels spawn in the seaweed beds of the Sargasso Sea in the Atlantic Ocean. They make long journeys to leave the sea for rivers, where they live for 30 years and more. Eels can survive for long periods out of water, protected by a coat of slime. This enables them to wriggle between wetland sites overland. Eventually, they return to the Sargasso Sea to breed.

Why are tidal wetlands important?

Tidal wetlands such as estuaries and mangrove forests provide important breeding sites and nurseries for some marine creatures. The vulnerable larvae and immature young of many species of fish and other marine creatures grow up in tidal wetlands. The wetlands provide many hiding places where they can avoid predators until they grow large enough to enter deeper waters.

Mangroves thrive in a bacteria-rich mud. The bacteria help decompose fallen mangrove leaves to form a thick, nutritious layer that feeds fish, shrimp, and other creatures. The wastes of these creatures then feed mollusks such as clams and water snails.

Dragonflies are common wetland insects. Female dragonflies lay their eggs on or near the water surface. Adult dragonflies hunt above the water, but their larvae live beneath the surface, where they ambush tadpoles and small fish.

Which insects live in fresh water?

Dragonflies and many other flying insects, including mosquitoes, lay their eggs in water or on the stems of water plants. The larvae that hatch from the eggs live underwater, sometimes for as long as two years, before emerging and changing into adults. Other insects, including several species of beetles, live permanently underwater. They breathe by capturing air from the surface and storing it under their wingcases.

What about spiders?

Water spiders need to breathe air, but they live and catch their prey underwater. They survive by making bell-shaped silk nets in which they capture air from the surface. They then anchor the nets to plant stems underwater. Water spiders also lay their eggs in these nets, and use them for storing prey. In Europe, the spiders live in ponds and ditches containing plenty of weeds, often in peaty upland regions.

How do amphibians use wetlands?

Wetlands are ideal habitats for amphibians. The word amphibian means "double life," because most species spend the first part of their lives beneath the water surface, and much of their adult lives on land (though they usually stay close to water). The most common amphibians are frogs and toads, but the group also includes newts, salamanders, and a group of legless amphibians called caecilians, which look like eels or large worms.

The tadpoles of wetland frogs and newts hatch from eggs laid in envelopes in the water (frogspawn or newt spawn). The tadpoles have gills, which allow them to breathe underwater. The tadpoles gradually change (metamorphose) into adults, which have lungs for breathing air. A common frog tadpole starts to gulp air from the surface at 8 to 10 weeks old, and leaves the water at about 16 weeks.

Even as adults, amphibians can survive for long periods underwater, as they can take in a certain amount of oxygen through their thin, moist skin. The need to keep this flexible skin moist is one of the things that makes wetlands perfect habitats for amphibians.

Frogs laying masses of frogspawn in shallow water. Frogs lay their spawn in great masses, whereas the common toad lays its eggs in long double strings.

Which reptiles depend on wetlands?

Reptiles such as crocodiles and turtles are among the planet's most successful species, and their success is due to their perfect adaptation to the wetlands they inhabit. Both turtles and crocodiles survived the global catastrophe that made the dinosaurs extinct, and both have lived ever since in swamps, rivers, ponds, and lakes.

The crocodile family includes alligators, caimans (a group of South American species), and gharials (fish-eating crocodiles with long, thin snouts). All of them have nostrils and eyes placed high on their skulls so that they can lay submerged but still watch for prey. Most live in warm climates, but some survive in cold waters in northern India and Nepal. These cold-water species sleep on river beds to avoid the coldest weather. They slow down their body processes, only surfacing now and then to breathe.

Crocodiles are efficient water-based predators. They hunt their prey, or wait to ambush it, either underwater, or almost totally concealed just beneath the surface.

Some aquatic turtles swim, and some walk along the bottom. All breathe with lungs, but they are also able to some extent to take in oxygen through their skins while they are submerged. Some species spend the winter underwater, and may not surface to breathe for weeks at a time.

Most snakes are good swimmers, and many enter water in pursuit of frogs and other prey. Some are semi-aquatic. The American cottonmouth moccasin lives in lowland swamps and streams, and feeds mainly on fish and amphibians. Some snakes hunt larger prey in rivers and swamps. The South American anaconda preys on caimans and turtles as well as mammals and birds, and can reach over 32ft (10m) in length.

Biomes WETLANDS 19

Migrating waterbirds such as these snow geese and sandhill cranes on a lake in New Mexico, depend on extensive wetlands. They need them both as breeding areas, and as stopover sites where they can rest and feed during their migration flights.

How useful are wetlands to birds?

Wetlands are essential to millions of water birds. Many species of geese, ducks, and shorebirds breed on the lakes and wetlands of northern Europe and Asia. As winter approaches and insect food supplies dwindle, huge flocks of birds migrate along long-established flyways to warmer regions in southern Europe, southern Asia, and Africa. Many stop over at wetland sites along the route, such as the French Camargue marshes, and the delta of the Danube River, to rest and feed before continuing their journey. Similar flocks migrate between the tundra areas of North America and warmer parts of South America.

How are birds adapted for wetland life?

Birds have adapted in a multitude of ways to wetland existence. Many, such as ducks, geese, and swans, have webbed feet to aid swimming. The long necks of swans enable them to reach food on the bottom three feet below the surface. Birds such as oystercatchers and curlews probe mud and sand for worms and shellfish. Different species have beaks of different lengths, depending on how deep their prey lives.

Many birds of prey hunt in wetlands. Some hunt other wetland birds, but some, such as fishing eagles and ospreys, have developed techniques for snatching fish from near the surface.

Do any mammals live in fresh water?

Few wetland mammals spend their entire lives in the water. Some that do are manatees and dugongs. Both species are distant relatives of elephants. These slow-moving plant-eaters have flippers and live in warm coastal shallows and rivers in the Americas and West Africa.

Freshwater dolphins are also completely aquatic. They are found in some Indian, Chinese, and South American rivers. River dolphins are smaller than their marine relatives, and they have longer snouts. The water in the rivers where these dolphins live is very cloudy, so the dolphins do not rely on eyesight to get around and find food. They get around using echolocation ("seeing" using sound), and find fish and crabs by probing the mud with their snouts.

River dolphins, such as these in the Amazon, spend their lives in fresh or brackish (slighty salty) water, where mud particles severely reduce visibility.

Which mammals need to live near water?

Hippos, the largest of the semi-aquatic mammals, spend their days in water, where they also mate and give birth. But at night, they leave their rivers to feed on vegetation. Capybaras are the South American equivalents of hippos.

Otters and beavers spend most of their lives in the water. Both species have webbed feet and are excellent swimmers. The beaver actually alters the nature of wetlands, by damming streams to create large ponds or lakes.

Several mammals hunt fish in the shallows of rivers, including jaguars and bears. The flat-headed cat of Southeast Asia is particularly adapted to the fish-eating life. It has a flat skull, very small ears, long, sharp upper teeth, and webbed toes. It is found in swamps, marshes, lakes, and forests flanking rivers. It feeds on fish, frogs, and shrimp, and puts its head completely underwater to snatch prey.

Who Are The Wetland Humans?

Very few people in today's world live in close harmony with wetland environments. This is because the wetlands themselves have been reduced or changed by modern technology. However, some communities still survive and live much as they have done for centuries, though most are under threat.

Reed boats on Lake Titicaca, on the border between Peru and Bolivia. Communities such as this depend on wetland resources such as fish and reeds.

LAKE TITICACA IS in the Andes mountains on the border between Bolivia and Peru. At over 12,500ft (3,800m) above sea level, it is the highest navigable lake on Earth. The lake is the home and the means of living for communities of native fishermen, hunters, and herders, some of whom live on floating islands of matted vegetation in the lake. They keep cattle, vicuñas (a kind of llama), and sheep on the shore.

They catch fish to eat and to sell, using boats made from bundles of the reeds that grow in large beds around the lake. Their houses are also made from reeds, and they use reeds to make handicrafts, which they sell. The way of life of these lake dwellers is beginning to change, and many now make most of their money by renting out rooms to tourists.

Netting a giant catfish on the Mekong River. Traditionally, Thai fishermen net the giant catfish of the Mekong River when it swims upstream to breed in the shallows.

On the other side of the world, the Marsh Arabs of Iraq also build boats and houses from reeds, and live on artificial floating islands. For 5,000 years, they have lived among the marshes and lakes of southern Iraq, fishing for food. In recent years, the fishermen have begun to switch from spears to nets, in order to catch more fish. They then sell the surplus fish in nearby towns.

The Marsh Arabs also prefer wooden or metal boats to reed boats now. Their way of life is greatly threatened, because in the last 25 years, about 90 percent of the marshes they depend on have been drained for irrigation and dams.

What about the Thai river villages?

Another community of wetland dwellers whose way of life is threatened live in Thailand along the Mekong River and its tributaries. The lives of local villagers are closely bound up with the seasonal cycles of the river and the hundreds of species of fish in it. Before each fishing season, the villagers perform religious ceremonies at favorite fishing spots. In April and May, until recently, the prize catch was always the giant catfish, caught as it swam upstream to spawn. These fish could weigh up to 660lbs (300kg). However, dams, and the dynamiting of rocky rapids, mean that the prize fish is threatened with extinction.

The villagers are also greatly dependant on wild plants and on vegetables cultivated in riverbank gardens and on mounds and small islands in the water. Over 100 local plants are used as herbs and for food. Some people make their living by gathering these plants and selling them.

Dams have already seriously affected water levels and movements of fish up the river. New plans to blast channels through rapids, to make it possible for boats to navigate the river, could disrupt traditional village life forever.

DEBATE—Are dams a good thing for local communities?

- Yes. They can store irrigation water for crops, and produce electricity for cities and villages. They make farming much more dependable, and provide valuable fisheries in the lakes behind the dams.
- No. Dams flood local food-growing areas and disrupt fish supplies.

How Do We Benefit From Wetlands?

Wetlands do not exist in isolation from the rest of the environment. They protect the land from the destructive force of seasonal floods and chemical build-ups, delivering nutrients to benefit plants and animals downstream, and producing crops of foods and materials.

WETLANDS TAKE THE pressure off rivers, especially during times of seasonal rains and thaws, which can overload river channels. Marshes, swamps, and lakes within the natural drainage basin of a river fill up in wet seasons. They hold a great deal of water that would otherwise drain into the main river channel and cause flooding.

Eventually, the wetlands release the extra water. Some may sink into the ground and become groundwater, held by underground rocks. Some may flow through the rock layers to enter other wetlands downstream. Some evaporates from wetland surfaces and becomes water vapor. Water also evaporates from the leaves of wetland plants—a process known as transpiration.

An aerial view of a river that has broken its banks, causing flooding. Flooding can be destructive, but it can also enrich the land. Wetlands can lessen the destructive power of floods by holding back excess water and then gradually releasing it.

A river's floodwaters may eventually reach regions of natural floodplain where they overflow the river's banks, but the "sponge" effect of upstream wetlands helps to keep these floods to manageable levels.

Deforestation, as here in Madagascar, can expose land to severe erosion. Seasonal rains wash huge quantities of earth down hillsides, producing deep rain channels (gullies) like these. Wetlands can help to absorb some of the sediments resulting from erosion, which would otherwise clog up the river channel.

How do wetlands trap pollution?

Wetlands can be effective traps for sediments. The sediments may be soil and rock particles eroded from hillsides and stream banks by heavy rain, or they may be the broken topsoils of agricultural land. River basin marshes and bogs are like shallow bowls with built-in filters and sponges. They trap sediments as they are carried toward the river in streams and flowing surface water. This helps prevent the river from having to carry too much sediment of its own, which could raise its bed and contribute to flooding.

The sediments that build up on the wetland floor can trap pollutants from factories and from farming. The pollutants become attached to particles of sediment, where they may gradually lose their harmful qualities.

Some poisonous heavy metals, such as copper, lead, and cadmium, may be absorbed and trapped by sedges (coarse grasses), bulrushes, cattails, and other wetland plants. The bacteria in wetland soils are also able to make some heavy metals nontoxic.

Rice needs a wet environment to thrive, and is planted throughout Asia in artificially flooded rice fields, or paddies. These rice paddies are in India.

How do wetlands help farmers?

As plants die off, they release many of the nutrients that have been feeding them back into the soil. Seasonal rains carry soil and nutrients into streams and rivers, which ferry them downstream. Many rivers have natural floodplains, where regular floodwaters spread across flat riverside land. Each time the land floods, soil particles mixed with plant nutrients are deposited as a layer of silt. The silt remains on the land as the floods recede and enriches the soil. Rice is a major floodplain crop, and the main food of some 3 billion people worldwide. Other food-producing wetland plants include coconut and oil palms, and the sago palm, which provides the basic food of many Southeast Asian communities.

What else do wetlands provide?

Aside from food, wetland plants can provide local people with a renewable supply of wood for building and fuel, as well as bark for leather tanning.

Wetland animal protein foods include fish, caught or farmed, waterbirds, mammals like the South American capybara, and reptiles such as alligators, which are hunted or bred for meat.

How do floods benefit grazing animals?

Floodplain grasslands provide vital grazing for both wild and domestic animals. On the floodplains of the Okavango Delta in Botswana, dry winter grasses grow on land that is flooded in the rainy season. These grasses are nourished by silt left behind from the floods. The grasses attract massive herds of large grazing mammals such as buffaloes, zebras, wildebeest, and impalas.

A Dinka child with a herd of cattle.

In the Sudd Marshes, which are within the floodplain of the White Nile, rich wetland grasses grow on the floodplain each year when the floods have receded. For many generations, herdspeople of the Dinka tribe have grazed their cattle on these grasses.

How do wetlands protect coasts?

Flood sediments carried down to estuaries and tidal flats provide essential nutrients for the many marine species that use them as nurseries. As we saw earlier (p. 17), these wetlands provide relatively well protected shallow waters where the young of marine species can develop, with less danger of being eaten by predators than in the open sea.

Mollusks such as oysters, clams, and mussels, and crustaceans such as crabs and shrimp, depend on tidal wetlands as breeding and feeding habitats.

Mangrove protection

There are almost 80 species of plants known as mangroves, and mangrove forests cover an area of some 69,500 sq mi (180,000 sq km) worldwide.

Wetland plants stabilize banks and shorelines, and bear the brunt of storms from the ocean, lessening their power further inland. The mangrove forests that occur along many tropical coasts provide important ocean defenses in regions where powerful storm surges are a real danger to low-lying coastal communities.

Do Human Activities Endanger Wetlands?

In the past, wetlands have had a bad public image. They were seen as wastelands, full of disease and danger. For centuries, governments have drained, leveled, and developed wetland areas for nonwetland uses such as intensive agriculture or the expansion of cities and industries. This "land reclamation" is still the biggest threat to wetlands.

The oil industry is a major polluter, responsible for the destruction of many freshwater wetlands and their wildlife. Oil spillages at sea also cause damage to tidal wetlands.

TODAY, WETLANDS COVER roughly 6 percent of the Earth's land area. This is about half the area that they originally covered. Most wetland loss has occurred since 1900. The worst losses ocurred in northern countries during the first half of the 1900s, but since 1950, tropical and subtropical wetlands have been lost at an increasing rate.

Drainage and clearance to make room for agriculture has been the main cause of wetland destruction. Some scientists estimate that by 1985, up to 65 percent of available wetlands in Europe and North America had been drained to make way for intensive agriculture. In Asia, the figure was 27 percent; in South America, 6 percent, and in Africa, 2 percent.

Shrimp farms like these in Thailand have become an important source of earnings for a number of poor countries. Cutting down mangroves to create shrimp ponds weakens shore storm defenses and disrupts the life cycles of many creatures.

In the US, wetland destruction has been almost total in some states. California has lost 91 percent of its original wetlands, and 21 other states have lost at least 50 percent. Almost all of the willow wetlands of the Rocky Mountains have given way to cattle grazing, housing developments, ski resorts, and agriculture. According to the US Fish and Wildlife Service, the wetlands are disappearing at a rate of about one acre every minute.

What is happening to mangrove forests?

Over 50 percent of the world's mangroves have disappeared in the last 20 years. They have been bulldozed to make room for marinas, hotels, airports, rice paddies, and shrimp ponds. Indonesia lost 665,000 acres of its mangroves between 1960 and 1990. Malaysia lost 580,000 acres between 1980 and 1990. Thailand lost 457,000 acres between 1960 and 1991. Practically all of these areas were replaced by shrimp farms. The Philippines, Bangladesh, Guatemala, Honduras, and Ecuador all cut down their mangroves and replaced them with shrimp ponds. In the process, they destroyed their coastal storm defenses, removed the rich mud that nurtured many marine creatures, and lost trees that delivered annual supplies of useful products.

DEBATE—Should mangroves be cleared to make way for shrimp farms?

- Yes. Shrimp can be exported, and make money for poor countries, which mangroves do not.
- No. Mangroves provide a regular supply of products for local villagers, but shrimp makes profits for a few businessmen.

How do we poison wetlands?

Wetlands can filter out or make harmless many chemicals that drain into them, but massive pollution can kill wetlands off. A large proportion of the fertilizers used by farmers to boost their crops eventually drain off the fields and are washed downstream to enter bogs, marshes, and lakes.

The nitrogen and phosphorus in this agricultural run-off stimulate the growth of plantlike organisms called algae—a process called eutrophication. The masses of algae cover the surface of standing or slow-moving water with a dense green blanket. This blocks off the light needed by more useful water plants. When the algae die and decompose, they remove the water's oxygen, so that it can support little plant or animal life.

Pesticides, and many household and industrial cleaners, contain chemicals that enter sewage and drainage systems, and find their way into wetlands, rivers, and finally the ocean. Many of these chemicals were designed to kill pests or bacteria, and can be very harmful to aquatic animals.

In many intensively cultivated agricultural regions, excess fertilizers have drained into wetlands, stimulating the growth of algae on the surface of ponds, lakes, and slow-flowing rivers.

Paper mills and other industrial plants on the shores of Russia's Lake Baikal have added toxic chemicals to the agricultural pesticides also flowing into the lake.

How is industry damaging wetlands?

Industrial chemicals are threatening the world's oldest and deepest lake. Lake Baikal in southern Siberia is at least 30 million years old. It is almost 440mi (700km) long, 50mi (80km) wide, and 5,370ft (1,637m) deep at its deepest point. Since the late 1950s, a paper pulp mill on the shores of the lake has been releasing poisonous chemicals made by pulp-bleaching into the lake's waters. DDT, a pesticide banned in much of the world, but still used in China, enters the lake from a river flowing into it from Mongolia, along with sewage and wastes from several cities.

Millions of tons of industrial chemicals and heavy metals also enter Lake Baikal from industries on its shore. At risk are more than 1,500 unique plant and animal species—including the world's only freshwater seal—which are found only in Lake Baikal. The sheer size of the lake has enabled it to survive these growing levels of pollution so far, but the seals, and some of the lake's unique fish species, are beginning to decrease in numbers.

Massive quantities of human sewage wastes can also overcome a wetland's natural cleaning capacities. The Lac de Tunis, outside the Tunisian capital, and the Manzalah lagoon outside Cairo have become cesspits for these major cities. Both are filled with stagnant water clogged with algae and able to support hardly any other life forms.

Biomes WETLANDS 31

What effects do dams have on wetlands?

Egypt's High Aswan Dam holds back the Nile waters. The nutritious silts once deposited annually by the river across its floodplain are now trapped in the artificial lake behind the dam. Also, the reduced flow of the river below the dam allows seawater to get into groundwater in the Nile Delta. However, the flooding of the Nile was never reliable; it often failed, or came late, or was excessive, and when these things happened, crops were destroyed.

Without the flood-silt, the farmers of the lower Nile floodplain need to use large amounts of chemical fertilizers to grow their crops (these are mainly cotton, rice, and sugar cane). The loss of silt has also affected major sardine fisheries beyond the Nile Delta, and the delta itself is rapidly shrinking.

DEBATE—Are dams a good thing for local communities?

- Yes. They can store irrigation water for crops, and produce electricity to use and sell. Electricity can also be brought to villages. They make farming much more dependable and provide valuable fisheries in the lakes behind the dams.
- No. Dams flood food-growing areas, disrupt fish movements, and provide electricity for cities, not villages.

The construction of Egypt's High Aswan Dam has provided power and reliable water supplies. However, it has also disrupted the river's flood cycles and caused the shrinking of the river delta.

The artificial lakes that form behind large dams, such as Lake Volta behind the Akosombo Dam in Ghana, permanently flood wetland systems upstream.

Traditional brick manufacturers, who used to use flood silt to make bricks, have had to move onto agricultural lands to excavate silts now that the floods have ceased.

There are more than 45,000 large dams worldwide (over 49ft [15m] high). In a large river system such as the Mekong River, the effects of dams are felt far upstream and downstream. Upstream, water levels rise to cover wetlands such as swamps, marshes, and river islands. Fish migrations are blocked, and damage is done to wildlife. Downstream, flooding depends on the opening or closing of the dam's sluices.

In 1995, China built the Man Wan Dam in Yunnan province, on the upper Mekong River. The fishermen of the Mekong's lower basin catch 1.75 million tons of fish each year, 20 percent of all the freshwater fish caught in the world. Since the building of the Man Wan Dam, fish catches have fallen drastically, because unpredictable changes in water level have disrupted the breeding behavior of many species.

In November, 2002, Chinese engineers plugged the final gap in the Three Gorges Dam on the Yangtze River. The dam, begun in 1993, is due to be completed in 2009. It will be 597ft (182m) high, have a reservoir 250mi (400km) long, and will displace an estimated 1.2 million people. On the other hand, it will also prevent the floods that once caused thousands of deaths and destroyed countless homes every few years.

How Does Wetland Degradation Affect Wildlife?

Animals that have adapted to wetland lifestyles are especially at risk from wetland degradation because of their adaptations. Without suitable wet conditions in which to breed, amphibians and wetland reptiles cannot survive. Also, migrating waterbirds need wetlands as stopover points on their long flights for rest and food.

THE EFFECT OF pollution on wetland wildlife is not always direct. Washed downstream, DDT and other pesticides strike first at the bottom of food chains, entering microscopic plant and animal organisms. Filter-feeding creatures such as worms and shellfish are the next in line, absorbing the long-lasting chemicals from the plankton on which they feed. Fish and birds feed on the worms and shellfish. At the top end of wetland food chains, birds of prey, dolphins, and seals feed on waterbirds and fish, and the entire accumulated load of poisons becomes lodged in their body fats and organs. The results can seriously affect their ability to breed, with birds of prey laying sterile eggs, and mammals dying from diseases because the chemicals damage their immune systems.

Large predators such as dolphins are at the top of wetland food chains. They can suffer from a deadly build-up of pollutants in their bodies.

Cranberries are a natural wetland plant, but commercial cranberry farms use large amounts of chemicals and heavy harvesting machinery, which exclude natural wildlife from the cranberry bogs.

How do oil spills affect wildlife?

Oil spills and illegal oil discharges are a particular threat to mangroves and the wildlife depending on them. Oil clogs the trees' breathing pores, and the roots become starved of oxygen. As the trees die off, they cease to provide the leaf-litter that mud bacteria need to make nutrients. Without the nutrients, fish and other marine creatures and their larvae cannot survive.

Why is intensive agriculture a threat?

Conversion of natural wetlands into intensive agricultural areas affects wildlife in more than one way. First, the natural habitat of many creatures is destroyed. Second, the intensive agriculture usually uses large quantities of chemicals. Pesticides draining out of the rice paddies of the Mekong Delta, for example, kill off crabs and other animals living in the delta mud.

Cranberries are a natural bog plant, but commercial cranberry bogs carved out of natural wetlands in Maine use chemical fertilizers and pesticides that repel any attempt by wildlife to return to its old habitats.

Industrial pollution sometimes leads to a total breakdown of wetland life systems. Smoke from industrial chimneys in parts of northern Europe mixes with rain clouds to fall as acid rain elsewhere on the continent. Over a fifth of Sweden's larger lakes now have a high acid content, and many Scandinavian lakes are crystal clear, because they are totally without plant or animal life. Living things cannot survive in the acid water.

A Florida panther in the Everglades. The panther is now close to extinction due to habitat loss and inbreeding. Panther support groups have had some success introducing panthers from outside the area to overcome the problems of inbreeding.

Which wetland animals are under threat?

According to the World Conservation Union (IUCN), over 800 animal species with close ties to wetlands are currently threatened with extinction. Wetland species cannot easily adapt to new environments.

In 1979, a large sea fish called the totoaba was declared endangered. The totoaba depended on the delta of the Colorado River, breeding in the mouth of the river. Tides carried the eggs up into the delta where they hatched. Unfortunately, almost all the waters of the river are now diverted for irrigation, leaving only a trickle at the river mouth. Other wildlife dependant on the delta, and becoming rarer, include the world's most endangered marine mammal, the vaquita porpoise, the brown pelican, and the delta clam.

The Florida panther, a subspecies of the cougar, has adapted to the swamp forests of the Florida Everglades. It suffers from a shrinking habitat as humans take more and more of the land. Loss of habitat also reduces prey numbers, and panthers are killed in road accidents.

Today, there are between 30 and 50 panthers surviving. The biggest danger to these survivors is inbreeding. Florida panthers have been isolated from other panther groups for over a century. Because the population is so tiny, it is inbred. Inbreeding leads to reduced fertility (which slows recovery of the population), heart abnormalities, and reduced immunity to disease. Without the introduction of mates from outside the area, the Florida panther will probably be extinct within 30 years.

How do changes affect migrating animals?

Unexpected changes in wetland terrains can be both confusing and deadly for migrating animals. Dams block the breeding and feeding movements of both fish and river dolphins in the Irrawaddy and Yangtze rivers. Filled ponds and ditches can remove the spawning grounds of amphibians such as toads and frogs. Migrating waterbirds can fail to reach their breeding and feeding grounds if the wetlands they use as stopovers have disappeared.

Manmade barriers can cause problems for wildlife. An incomplete canal bed across the Sudd Marshes produced a barrier that migrating grazers cannot cross. In the James Bay region of Quebec, Canada, 10,000 migrating caribou were drowned in 1984 when sluice gates were opened on a hydroelectric dam upstream from their migratory route.

DEBATE—Does it matter if a rare animal species becomes extinct?

- Yes. All living creatures are important, and all species contribute to the health and balance of the environment.
- No. It is a waste of time and money trying to keep some creatures from becoming extinct, especially if they are of no use to humans.

Artificial obstacles such as this oil pipeline in the Alaskan Arctic may cut across the traditional migration routes of caribou herds, which travel thousands of miles north and south each year.

How Do The Changes To Wetlands Affect Humans?

Housing, airports, or rice fields seem much more important to growing human populations, desperate for space, than marshes or swamps. Unfortunately, changing a wetland into a human facility often solves one problem in the short term but creates a host of others in the long term.

The generating room of a hydroelectric power station. Hydroelectric power is a clean way of generating electricity. It has benefited many countries by producing power for homes and industries.

MODERN TOWNS AND industries need huge supplies of electricity to keep them going. They, and their supporting agriculture, also use huge supplies of water. Large dams and hydroelectric generation are an obvious way of meeting these demands. Hydroelectricity provides some 19 percent of the world's electricity.

What are the costs of dams?

However, in the developing world, dams flood the lands of many wetland communities. Up to 80 million people worldwide have been displaced by large dams. In India alone, 20–30 million have lost their homes and lands to dams in the last 50 years. These people are uprooted, and often have to move to areas where there is no work. They rarely benefit from the electricity generated by the dams, most of which is sold to industry, or goes to major towns.

Sometimes no one benefits from the building of a dam except the dam contractors. Completed in 1960, China's Sanmenxia Dam across the Yellow River displaced 300,000 people. Within two years of completion, the reservoir had filled with silt, rendering the dam useless. Dynamited and rebuilt twice since then, it still has to be emptied of silt each winter.

Can non-native species affect wetlands?

Humans annually consume 30 million tons of freshwater fish. Despite this dependence, many freshwater fish-stocks have been depleted through human activity, depriving fishing communities of both food and work. Pollution and water diversion contribute to the fall in numbers of freshwater fish.

In some places, fish that do not belong there have been introduced into wetland areas. This can be catastrophic. In 1960, for example, the Nile perch, which can weigh up to 440lbs (200kg), was introduced into Lake Victoria. It soon started eating the small fish that naturally lived in the lake. These fish were the basis of the fishing industry in the area. By the 1980s, up to 200 species of native fish were extinct. The locals used to wind-dry the small fish, but this is impossible with the large perch. It has to be cooked in its own oil, using large amounts of firewood. Deforestation of islands and lake shores is occurring as a result. The Lake Victoria fisheries may collapse due to overfishing.

The Nile perch can grow to an enormous size in lakes where it has been introduced artificially, mainly by eating the native fish species. What at first seemed a good commercial move has sometimes ended up as an ecological disaster.

Oil plants on the Niger Delta have caused illness and death for many local people, due to the pollution of earth and water by dumped and spilled oil and oil sludges.

How is wetland damage ruining lives?

The destruction or degradation of a wetland can totally disrupt the lives of those depending on it. The reservoirs of dams drown villages, and pollution can make wetlands uninhabitable, forcing wetland communities to move out.

Since 1956, the Nigerian government has allowed the Shell Oil Company to extract oil in the Niger Delta. The government receives large amounts of money for this oil, but there have been consequences for communities living in the delta. Oil spills and the dumping of oil waste have polluted soils and water systems. Pipeline explosions and polluted water have killed many people. With their farms ruined by pollution, thousands of villagers have left their homes and farmlands and moved to the town of Port Harcourt. They have become refugees in their own country.

The refugees fleeing wetland destruction come from farming, herding, and fishing communities. With no means of earning a living with their traditional skills, they almost always move to the outskirts of towns, where they may be able to find casual laboring work. Their village culture is disrupted, probably forever.

Environmental refugees

According to the Red Cross, around 58 percent of the world's 43 million refugees have left their homes due to disasters in their environments. In eight years, according to the UN Environmental Program, there could be 50 million environmental refugees, many from destroyed wetlands.

Can wetland destruction raise sea levels?

The destruction of wetlands can lead to an increase in so-called greenhouse gases. The main greenhouse gas is carbon dioxide. It and other greenhouse gases form a layer in the atmosphere that acts like the glass in a greenhouse, trapping much of the Sun's heat near the Earth's surface. The gases released when factories burn fuels and the exhaust gases from cars have increased the amounts of greenhouse gases in the atmosphere. Most scientists think that this is causing the Earth to get warmer—a process known as global warming.

Many wetlands, especially those with peat deposits, act as "sinks" that hold on to carbon dioxide. When peat bogs are dug up, or allowed to dry out, they release carbon dioxide into the air. This increases global warming.

There is strong evidence that global warming is melting polar ice and causing sea levels to rise. For instance, in March, 2002, the 500 million billion ton Larsen B ice-shelf in Antarctica collapsed into the ocean, and this was seen by some as a sign of global warming.

Many low-lying islands are already threatened by rises in sea levels. It is forecast that over the next 100 years, sea levels could rise by 3ft (1m). In Bangladesh, which is already prone to flooding, such a rise in sea level would flood 10 million people out of their homes.

Low-lying Pacific islands are in danger of being submerged as sea levels begin to rise due to global warming.

What Are We Doing About Wetland Destruction?

Many people have been aware of the dangers facing wetlands for a long time, but there now seems to be a growing sense of urgency. An increasing number of organizations, many of them independent of governments, are doing research and giving publicity to the problems. In some countries, local people have started to organize protests against projects such as dams.

The Coto Doñana National Park is an important wetland site that is endangered by tourist developments and industrial pollution.

THE RAMSAR CONVENTION on Wetlands, set up in 1971, is an international conservation agreement. It brings governments and independent organizations together to consider wetland problems. One of its best-known activities is the establishment of particular Ramsar sites for governments to maintain and protect. All its recommendations are voluntary, and although there are about 1,200 Ramsar sites worldwide, many remain at risk, with governments taking little or no protective action.

One of the best ways to ensure the survival of wetlands and other natural environments is to teach children their importance by giving them first hand, onsite experience.

Independent organizations concerned with general wildlife welfare, or with general environmental protection, often campaign on wetland issues. Probably the best known is WWF (World Wildlife Fund, now known as the Worldwide Fund for Nature), which was set up as a charity in 1961. WWF is one of the largest independent conservation organizations, with 5 million supporters and 28 national organizations. One of WWF's early campaigns was to raise money to buy a section of the Guadalquivir Marshes in Spain. This area was an important wetland habitat, and a stopover point for millions of migrating birds. In 1969, with the help of the Spanish Government, WWF bought the land and set up the Coto Doñana National Park, an important European wetland site. WWF is currently campaigning against the drainage of water from the marshes for irrigation and to service tourist facilities.

Other independent organizations whose work covers wetland issues include the International Conservation Union (IUCN), Friends of the Earth, Greenpeace, and the Nature Conservancy. All of these organizations issue large amounts of information and publicity through leaflets, magazine articles, and websites, as well as carrying out education programs and conservation activities in the field. On the whole, they remain free of the influence of governments and large corporations.

The IUCN worked with the World Bank in the temporary World Commission on Dams in 1999 and 2000. The World Bank has funded large numbers of controversial dams in developing countries, but one of the conclusions of the World Commission on Dams was that dams "have made an important and significant contribution to human development, but in too many cases, the social and environmental costs have been unacceptable, and often unnecessary." Most environmental groups are hostile to dam building.

A growing number of wildlife TV programs have introduced the beauties—and the problems—of wetland regions into millions of homes.

How can television help wetlands?

Increasing the public's awareness of the problems is one of the most important goals of the wetland conservationist. Television has played a major part in this. There are a large number of very popular and well-made TV programs and series about wildlife and the environment. There is often an illustrated book that goes with the series. However, it takes more than programs and illustrated books to convince governments that they should be doing something about wetlands.

Can direct action work?

In many countries, taking direct action against official policies is risky, but it sometimes works. For many years, fishing communities in the Mekong Delta demonstrated, marched, and even occupied public buildings in their fight against the damming of the Mun tributary. They were beaten, abused, and sometimes imprisoned, but in the end, the authorities agreed to open the sluice gates of the dam during the breeding season of the fish. Right away, the migratory fish began to pass through the dam to breed upstream, and the villagers began to catch fish again as they had for centuries.

Protesters will go to great lengths to demonstrate their opposition to dams when they realize that their entire way of life is under threat. Thousands of Indians have protested for years against the damming project on the Narmada River, which will displace them from their villages and lands forever.

Are governments helping?

In the end, governments make the decisions, and some of their decisions have helped wetlands. Many countries have now banned the use of DDT and similar pesticides, after it was discovered that they were a danger to humans as well as to some animals. Governments have also established fines for oil tankers that release oil into the sea and break safety regulations. Unfortunately, many tanker owners are prepared to risk a fine, and continue to wash out their oil tanks at sea illegally. They also use dangerously old and battered vessels. An example is the tanker *Prestige*, which broke up and sank off the Spanish coast in November, 2002, carrying with it 70,000 tons of heavy oil. This disaster has persuaded the governments of France, Spain, Portugal, and Italy to try to persuade the rest of the European Union to ban aging, single-hulled tankers from EU waters in the future.

One area in which progress has been made in the fight to persuade governments to care for wetlands is the replanting of mangroves. In Pakistan, the IUCN (The International Conservation Union) and the Sindh Forest Department finished a 10-year replanting scheme in the Indus Delta in 1997.

Conservation and replanting work began in both Florida and Queensland, Australia after realizing that 90 percent of their commercial fish stocks depended on the mangroves. In China, plans were announced early in 2002 to increase mangrove areas from 60,800 acres to 209,000 acres by 2010.

Where Do We Go From Here?

Where wetlands are concerned, all problems are urgent. Wildlife habitats are under threat and species are in danger of extinction. Human wetland communities are being displaced permanently, and their cultures disrupted. Freshwater supplies are dwindling while water demand is increasing.

Crowded cities are a hostile environment for refugees who have been displaced from their villages by dams and drainage schemes.

WETLAND CAMPAIGNERS continue to lobby governments and industry with scientific arguments showing why wetlands should be conserved or repaired. They also continue educating the public about wetland degradation. Meanwhile, it is possible that a further argument, closer to politicians' hearts, will make an impact. Wetland destruction costs governments money. Some of these costs are obvious. Cleaning up a major oil spill is expensive, but has to be done because of the tourist industry as well as the wildlife. Dams cost a fortune to build, and sometimes do not produce enough electricity to cover their costs.

Freshwater fish being sold in a Thai market. Village life, based on small-scale production of food which is then sold locally, can enable villagers to live a productive and secure life. It is also favorable as a healthy environment.

Environmental refugees present another kind of financial burden. People who are moved to make way for a reservoir, or whose livelihood is destroyed by the draining of wetlands, flock to towns seeking jobs. The ever-increasing numbers of such refugees mean that cities need extra food, water, housing, jobs, transportation, and medical care. Faced with ever larger bills for keeping their cities running, governments may begin to think that it was better when villagers lived in self-supporting communities, growing their own vegetables, tending their own animals, and catching their own fish. As villagers, they created money, selling produce, fish, and wild herbs. As environmental refugees, they cost money.

The future for many wetlands is perilous. Politicians often do not have the time or the energy to think about rare deer or endangered trees. By themselves, the rarities and the fragile habitats earn neither money nor votes.

But wetlands fit into a larger picture, and much of the information coming from scientists and teachers stresses that species and environments should be seen as parts of this larger whole. Everything has its role to play, and the health of the whole depends on the health of the parts.

DEBATE—Are small wetland communities a thing of the past?

- Yes. Young people do not want to live the old life, and cities provide them with excitement as well as modern jobs.
- No. Village life is healthier, and the old skills of fishing and growing food are useful and valuable.

REFERENCE

AREA OF FRESHWATER WETLANDS

Continent	Area of wetlands (acres)
Africa	300,000,000 to 308,100,000
Asia	504,700,000
Eastern Europe	566,400,000
Neotropics	1 billion
North America	597,000,000
Oceania	88,340,000
Western Europe	71,200,000
Total	3 to 4 billion

(Source: Wetlands International and the Environmental Research Institute of the Supervising Scientist, Australia, for the Ramsar Convention, 1998)

USE OF WETLANDS

Continent	Percentage of wetlands drained
Europe*	56–65
North America*	56–65
Asia	27
South America	6
Africa†	2

* By 1985, an estimated 56–65% of the available wetland in Europe and North America had been drained for intensive agriculture.
† More than 50 developing countries, especially in Africa, use less than 1% of their annual renewable freshwater resources.

FRESH WATER

- Global consumption of fresh water is doubling every 20 years.

- According to the UN, in 1996 we used around 54% of all accessible freshwater from lakes, rivers, and other sources.

- By 2025, our use of fresh water is expected to rise to 70%.

- About 70% of the water we use goes to grow food. This rises to 95% in parts of North Africa, Asia, and the US.

- Underground aquifers (stores of groundwater) are being depleted in some areas 10 times faster than they can refill themselves.

- Some Chinese water tables are being lowered at the rate of 5ft (1.5m) every year.

- In Tamil Nadu, India, many aquifers are now dry. Other aquifers in the area have dropped 98ft (30m) in as many years.

- In the 1980s, Central America achieved a 32% increase in agricultural production but used 200% more pesticides. Residues from some of these pesticides find their way into water supplies.

HUMAN USE OF FRESH WATER

Country or area	Water used per person per year (cubic feet)
World average	23,000
Industrialized countries	42,400
United States	74,100
Burkina Faso, Congo, Burundi, Guinea Bissau, Zaire	less than 900

(Source: Manager Freshwater Ecosystems Program of WWF International, 1998)

Mangrove Species

- There are up to 80 species of mangroves worldwide, covering an area of 69,500 sq mi (180,000 sq km).

- The northernmost limit of mangroves is the Kyushu Islands, Japan (35°N). The southernmost limit is Auckland, New Zealand (37°S).

- *Rhizophora* spp.—roots arch above water; pores supply oxygen to submerged roots.

- *Avicennia* spp.—slim, vertical "breathing roots" called pneumatophores.

- *Bruguiera* spp.—trunks that widen at the base and kneelike pneumatophores.

Mangrove Losses

- Thailand: 457,000 acres lost 1960–91, to shrimp ponds.

- Malaysia: 580,000 acres lost 1980–90, to shrimp ponds and agricultural clearance.

- Indonesia: 665,000 acres lost 1960–90, to shrimp ponds.

- Vietnam: 257,000 acres lost 1960–74, to US Army defoliants.

- Philippines: 420,000 acres lost 1967–76, mainly to shrimp ponds.

- Bangladesh: 183,000 acres lost since 1975, mainly to shrimp ponds.

- Guatemala: 23,500 acres lost 1965–84, to shrimp ponds and salt farming.

Dams

- Worldwide, there are over 40,000 dams over 49ft (15m) high. China has 1,900 and the US has 5,500.

- From 1950 to 1970, 1,000 dams were built each year.

- Since the early 1990s, about 260 dams have been built each year.

- The countries with the most dams being built are China, Turkey, South Korea, and Japan.

- According to the World Commission on Dams, 40–80 million people have been displaced by dams in the last 50 years; 75% of those displaced in India have not been resettled.

- Currently, about 2 million people are being displaced each year by large dams.

Hydroelectricity

- Hydroelectric power provides 19% of the world's electricity. About 20% of China's electricity comes from hydroelectric power; 75% comes from coal.

Hydroelectric Power Production

Region	Production in 2001 (billion kilowatt hours)
North America	565
Central & South America	513
Western Europe	514
Eastern Europe	272
Middle East	14
Africa	73
Asia and Oceania	580
World total	over **2.5 billion**

(Source: US Government official statistics)

Methane

- Also known as marsh gas, methane is produced wherever organic material decomposes. Ice-core analysis shows it to have been present in the atmosphere at a concentration of 0.7 parts per million by volume (ppmv) for the 2000 years up to 1800.

- Since then, concentrations have almost doubled, and are increasing at around 0.6% per year. Current atmospheric concentration is around 2 ppmv.

- The greenhouse effect of a molecule of methane is 7.5 times that of a molecule of carbon dioxide. Wetlands form the main source of natural methane.

- Methane's atmospheric life is about 12 years, much shorter than that of carbon dioxide.

- The growth in atmospheric methane closely follows the growth of the human population since the Industrial Revolution.

Methane Estimates

Source	Amount (millions of tons per year)
Wetlands	115
Fossil fuel industry	100
Rice paddies	60

GLOSSARY

acidic Containing acid.

agricultural To do with farming.

algae Tiny, aquatic, plantlike organisms that sometimes blanket the surface of stagnant (still) or slow-flowing water. .

amphibian Vertebrates (animals with backbones) that spend some time on land but need water in which to breed and grow to adulthood.

aquatic Living or growing in water.

aquifer A layer of soil or rock that can hold large amounts of water.

bacteria Microscopic single-celled living things. Some kinds are responsible for decay.

basin A bowl-shaped dip or depression in the ground.

caiman A South American reptile, similar to a crocodile or alligator.

dam An artificial barrier that holds back a river.

degraded Damaged or reduced in quality.

delta A fan-shaped region at a river's mouth.

deposit A layer of a substance left by a liquid.

emergent Waterside plant with its root in the water and most of its stem above the surface.

estuary The mouth of a river: the part that is tidal.

evaporation The process by which a liquid becomes a gas.

fen A peaty marsh that is low in acidity.

fertilizer A substance added to soil to help plants to grow.

floodplain A flat land flanking a river, which floods in the rainy season.

fresh water Water that is not salty, such as that in rivers, lakes, and marshes.

geological fault A fracture in a bed of rocks.

gharial A fish-eating Indian crocodile.

greenhouse gas A gas in the atmosphere (most commonly carbon dioxide) that traps the Sun's heat and warms up the Earth's surface.

habitat The natural environment of a plant or animal.

inbreeding Breeding between closely related animals.

irrigate To supply with water through channels or pipes.

larva The immature early stage of an insect, amphibian, or fish.

lobby To put your point of view to the government or other officials.

mangrove One of several kinds of trees that can grow in water.

migratory Making seasonal journeys between regions to breed or to escape an unsuitable climate.

mollusk An invertebrate (an animal without a backbone) with a soft body, usually having a shell.

monsoon The wind that brings the rainy season in India and Southeast Asia.

navigable A river or other stretch of water along which large boats or ships can travel.

nutrient A nourishing substance.

organic chemical A chemical compound based on carbon.

peat A spongy, wet soil made from rotted plant material.

pesticide A poison used to kill weeds, or insects and other crop pests.

pneumatophore Breathing organs of certain kinds of mangroves.

pollution The process of harming a natural area of soil, air, or water with chemicals or waste products.

prey An animal that is hunted for food by another animal.

rapids Fast, shallow river waters, usually running over rocks.

reaches Stretches of river.

rice paddy Artificial flat area that is flooded for part of the year for growing rice.

sedge A coarse kind of grass.

sediment A substance that settles at the bottom of a liquid.

silt A fine-grained sediment.

sluice-gate A gate that controls water flow through an opening in a dam.

spawn The egg mass of a fish or amphibian.

spawning The laying of spawn.

species A group of animals or plants that are very similar.

tidal Regularly covered by tides.

toxic Poisonous.

transpiration The process by which plants lose water from their leaves.

tributary A stream or river that runs into a larger flow.

tundra Bleak, flat lands close to the Arctic. In the tundra, the soil is frozen for most of the year.

wetland A region that is a combination of land, water, plants and, usually, animals.

FURTHER INFORMATION

BOOKS

Wetlands by Max Finlayson and Mike Moser (International Waterfowl and Wetlands Research Bureau, 1991)
A little out of date, but extremely comprehensive and well illustrated with photographs and maps.

Habitats—Wetlands by Ewan McLeish (Wayland, 1995)
An accessible book that is involving for children. Good explanations of wetland processes.

Fish—An Enthusiast's Guide by Peter B. Moyle (UCAL Press, 1993)
Half an academic book and half popular science, this book is very good on extinctions and near-extinctions.

The Dammed by Fred Pearce (Bodley Head, 1992)
One of the best books around on the politics of dams, by one of Britain's foremost environmental writers.

"The Greater Common Good." Essay in the collection *The Algebra of Infinite Justice* by Arundhati Roy (Flamingo, 2002)
A passionate and riveting description of the long fight against the dam planned for the Narmada Valley in India.

Climate Change by Simon Scoones (Wayland, 2001)
Graphic explanations of our changing climate.

MAGAZINES

National Geographic
A monthly magazine covering new discoveries about animals, plants and habitats, with extensive coverage of conservation issues – including those involving wetlands.

WDCS Magazine
The quarterly magazine of the Whale and Dolphin Conservation Society. Full of stunning pictures, but you have to join the Society to get it. Well worth it.

The Ecologist
Excellent articles on all aspects of conserving the planet, including articles on wetlands.

ORGANIZATIONS

WWF-USA
1250 24th Street N.W.
P.O. Box 97180
Washington, D.C. 20090-7180
www.worldwildlife.org

Friends of the Earth
1025 Vermont Avenue, N.W.
Suite 300
Washington, D.C. 20005
www.foe.org

Greenpeace
702 H Street N.W.
Suite 300
Washington, D.C. 20001
www.greenpeaceusa.org

The Nature Conservancy
4245 North Fairfax Drive
Suite 100
Arlington, VA 22203-1606
www.nature.org

Survival International
6 Charterhouse Buildings,
London EC1M 7ET
UK
www.survival-international.org

WEBSITES

http://mbgnet.mobot.org/fresh/
The wetlands section of the website Biomes of the World, with information on the plant and animal life of rivers, lakes, marshes, and other wetlands.

http://www.wetlands.org/
The Wetlands International website. Wetlands International is a global nonprofit organization dedicated to the conservation and sustainable management of wetlands. The site includes maps showing the Ramsar Convention wetlands sites around the world.

www.iucn.org/themes/wetlands
www.worldwildlife.org
The websites of the IUCN and WWF. Both websites contain virtually limitless amounts of information on wetlands, among other things. Both produce excellent profiles on particular wetland sites, wetland wildlife species, individual countries, and campaigns, as well as detailing their own extensive involvement in education and international conservation work.

http://www.nwrc.usgs.gov/
Website of the US Geological Survey's National Wetlands Research Center. The site includes news, fact sheets, and educational materials.

http://www.nwf.org/wetlands/
The wetlands pages of the US National Wildlife Federations website.

INDEX

acid rain 35
alewives 16
algae 30, 52
alligators 19, 26
Amazon River 8
 dolphins 21
Amazon water lily 14
amphibians 18, 34, 37, 52
anaconda 19
Andes Mountains 22
animals 14, 31, 36
Aswan Dam, Egypt 5, 32
Australia 10, 45

bald cypress 6
bears 21
beavers 21
beetles 17
billabongs 10
birds 14, 20, 26, 34, 37
bladderworts 15
bogs 12, 13, 25, 30, 35
Brahmaputra River 9
bulrushes 25

Camargue 20
capybara 21, 26
carbon dioxide 41
carnivorous plants 15
catfish 16, 23
cats 21
China 5, 31, 33, 39, 45
clams 17, 27, 36
coastal wetlands 7, 11
coconut 26
Colorado River 36
conservation 42, 43, 44, 45
Coto Doñana National
 Park 42, 43
crabs 27
cranberries 35
Cree Indians 5
crocodiles 19
crustaceans 27
curlews 20
cypress trees 6, 8, 15

Danube River 20
DDT 31, 34, 45
decomposition 12
deforestation 25, 39
degradation 34, 40, 46
deltas 7, 11, 12, 52
deposits 12, 13, 52
Dinka tribe 27
dolphins 21, 34, 37
dragonflies 17
drainage 28, 43, 46
ducks 20
duckweeds 15
dugongs 21
dynamiting 4, 23, 39

eels 16
Egypt 5, 32
elephants 9
emergent plants 13, 52
erosion 12, 13, 25
estuaries 7, 11, 17, 27, 52
eutrophication 30
evaporation 7, 10, 24, 52
Everglades 6, 8, 36

fens 7, 52
fertilizers 5, 30, 32, 35, 52
fishermen 4, 5, 22, 33
fishing eagles 20
flood-control systems 10
Florida 45
 Everglades 6, 8, 36
food chains 34
forests 7, 14
Friesian Islands 9
frogs 18, 37

Ganges River 9
geese 20
geological faults 9, 52
global warming 12, 41
grasses 8, 9, 15, 27
grasslands 9, 26
greenhouse gases 41, 52
groundwater 24, 32

habitat loss 36
hippos 21
hydroelectric power 4, 37, 38, 39

Indus Delta 45
insects 14, 15, 17
Irrawaddy River 37
irrigation 23, 32, 36, 43, 52

jaguars 21
James Bay, Canada 5, 37

lagoons 7
Lake Baikal 31
Lake Okeechokee 8
Lake Titicaca 22
Lake Victoria 39

Madagascar 25
Malaysia 29
mammals 9, 14, 21, 26, 34
Man Wan Dam 33
manatees 21
mangrove forests 6, 9, 17
mangroves 7, 8, 11, 15, 27, 29, 35, 45
Markham River, Papua New Guinea 7
Marsh Arabs 23
marsh plants 13
marshlands 8
meanders 13
Mekong River 4, 5, 9, 16, 23, 33, 44
mercury poisoning 5
metals 25, 31
methane gas 12
minerals 7
mollusks 17, 27, 53
monsoon rains 10, 11, 53
mosquitoes 17

mosses 12
mud 7, 12, 15, 17, 29, 35
mudflats 11
mussels 27

newts 18
Niger Delta 40
Nile perch 39
Nile River 5, 9, 10, 27, 32
Northern Territory, Australia 10

oil 28, 35, 40, 45, 46
Okavango Delta 6, 9, 13, 26
ospreys 20
otters 21
oxbow lakes 13
oxygen 35
oystercatchers 20
oysters 27

paddies 26, 29, 35
panhandle 9, 13
Pantanal 8
panther 36
Papua New Guinea 7
peat 6, 7, 12, 13, 41, 53
pesticides 30, 31, 34, 35, 45, 53
plants 6, 14, 15, 31
    decomposition 12
    succession 12
pollution 25, 28, 30, 31, 34, 39, 40, 42, 53
ponds 15, 19

Quebec, Canada 5, 37
Queensland, Australia 10, 45

rainfall 7, 12
rainy season 8, 9
Ramsar Convention 42
reclamation 28

reeds 7, 15, 22, 23
reptiles 19, 26, 34
rice 26, 29, 32, 35, 38, 53
river dolphins 21, 37
rivers 12
    estuaries 7
    flooding 7, 11, 24, 25
    mammals 21
    marshes 7
    nutrients 26
    Pantanal 8
    reptiles 19
Rocky Mountains 29
royal Bengal tiger 9
rushes 7, 15

sago palm 26
salmon 16
salt lakes 7
salt marshes 7, 9, 11
salt water 7, 15, 16
sandbanks 9, 11
sea 7, 11
seals 31, 34
sedges 8, 15, 25, 53
sediment 12, 15, 25, 27, 53
Severn Estuary, UK 11
sewage 30, 31
Shell Oil Company 40
shorebirds 20
shrimp farms 29
silt 7, 13, 26, 32, 33, 39
snakes 19
soil 25, 26
spiders 17
storm surges 11, 27
streams 8, 12, 26
succession 12
Sudd Marshes 9, 10, 27, 37
Sunderbans 9
sundew plant 12, 15
swamp cypress 15
swamp forest 6, 7, 11
swamps 6, 7, 11, 13, 24
    Australia 10

cypress 8
mammals 21
Okavango 9
reptiles 19
Sudd 10
swans 20

tadpoles 17, 18
Thailand 4, 23, 29, 47
Three Gorges Dam 5, 33
tidal flats 7, 9, 11, 15, 27
tidal wetlands 9, 11, 17, 28
tides 7, 9, 36
tigers 9
toads 18, 37
tourists 42, 43, 46
transpiration 24, 53
trees 6, 7, 14, 15
tundra 20, 53
turtles 19

United Kingdom 11
United States 6, 29, 35, 45

Wadden Sea 9
water hyacinths 15
water lilies 14, 15
water snails 17
waterholes 10
waterweed 15
White Nile River 9, 10, 27
WWF 43

Yangtze River 5, 33, 37
Yellow River 39